זְמַן לָשִׁיר

TIME TO SING HEBREW

ORIGINAL SONGS FOR CHILDREN

COMPOSED BY

FRAN AVNI

A.R.E. PUBLISHING
DENVER, COLORADO

ACKNOWLEDGEMENTS

Grateful thanks are due to:

Dr. Orna Lenchner, the originator of *Kadimah!: Get Ready for Hebrew!* and *Z'man Likro: Time To Read Hebrew*, for her invaluable input. Her suggestions and energy were a constant inspiration.

Stephen Glass, a talented young musician whose experience in Jewish music, conducting, and arrangement greatly enriched this project. (He is responsible for the lovely chord changes, and wonderful keyboard playing on the recording.)

Hillary Zana, for the excellent teaching guide at the back of this Songbook, which contains suggestions for using the *Z'man LaShir* cassette in the classroom.

Rivka Dori, who served as Hebrew Consultant during this project.

Dina Maiben, whose lyrics for *"Lo Kol Yom Purim"* were a joy to work with.

My colleague, Stephen Melzack, who contributed to the good morning feel of *"Boker Tov."*

A.R.E. Publishing, Inc. – Audrey Friedman Marcus and Rabbi Raymond A. Zwerin – for their encouragement and support throughout.

Music engraving: Sylvie Allard
Front cover photo: Jackie Cytrynbaum
Cover design: Hal Aqua

PREFACE

It was a unique challenge to create a music component for the two exciting Hebrew programs originated by Dr. Orna Lenchner, *Kadimah!: Get Ready for Hebrew!* and *Z'man Likro: Time To Read Hebrew*. Working with a select vocabulary and specific language patterns, I was able to create musically interesting material while maintaining the integrity of the teaching concepts. The result is catchy tunes, snappy lyrics, and rhythms that appeal to children as well as to teachers.

The songs on the *Z'man LaShir* cassette are based on the Key Words found in the five units of *Kadimah!*, the reading readiness program produced by A.R.E. Publishing, and on songs that illustrate some of the vocabulary in *Z'man Likro*, the primer that follows it. For using *Z'man LaShir* with *Kadimah!* and *Z'man Likro*, refer to the teaching guide which begins on page 51 of this Songbook. (These songs can also be used with any other Hebrew reading readiness program or primer.)

These 14 original compositions are sure to provide active, light-hearted, lively language learning, with singable syntax, vivid vocabulary, and painless pronunciation practice. They are meant for use in early childhood classrooms, in supplementary schools, as reinforcement/review for day school students. The songs are also ideal for home use, providing an enjoyable introduction to Hebrew vocabulary and concepts for the whole family. The eclectic musical styles, ranging from ragtime to bluegrass, will interest music teachers, Cantors, and songleaders, as well as language learners of all ages.

Kadimah! – Z'man Lashir Ivrit! It's Time To Sing Hebrew!

Fran Avni

CONTENTS

KEY TO TRANSLITERATION

a	as in car
ai	as in sigh
e	as in fed
eh	as in they
i	as in pin or me
o	as in form
'	as in it
cȟ	as in Bach

Z'MAN LIKRO
(Time To Read Hebrew)

Words and Music: Fran Avni

F G F G C Fine
Z'man z'man z'man ka - di - mah Z'man li - kro Iv - rit
Instrumental
C G/C F/C G/C C G/C F/C G/C
Verse
C C/E F C/E F C D7 G
A - leph Bet Gi - mel Da - led Hey Vav Za - yin Chet Tet Yod
C C7 F C/E F C/E D G7
Kaph La-med Mem Nun Sa-mech A-yin Pey Tsa - di Koph Resh Shin v' - Tav.
C C7 F C C G C
Twen-ty-two le-tters and that's e-nough Z'man li - kro li - kro Iv - rit
D.S. al fine
C C7 F C C G C
Twen-ty-two le-tters and that's e-nough Z'man li - kro li - kro Iv - rit.

זְמַן לִקְרֹא Z'MAN LIKRO
(TIME TO READ HEBREW)

זְמַן (3x)	*Z'man, z'man, z'man*
זְמַן לִקְרֹא עִבְרִית	*Z'man likro Ivrit.*
זְמַן (3x)	*Z'man, z'man, z'man*
קָדִימָה	*Kadimah -*
זְמַן לִקְרֹא עִבְרִית	*Z'man likro Ivrit.*
אָלֶף, בֵּית, גִּימֶל, דָּלֶת,	*Aleph, Bet, Gimel, Daled,*
הֵא, וָו, זַיִן,	*Hey, Vav, Zayin,*
חֵית, טֵית, יוֹד,	*Chet, Tet, Yod,*
כָּף, לָמֶד, מֵם, נוּן,	*Kaph, Lamed, Mem, Nun,*
סָמֶךְ, עַיִן, פֵּא,	*Samech, Ayin, Pey,*
צָדִי, קוֹף, רֵישׁ,	*Tsadi, Koph, Resh*
שִׁין וְ־תָו.	*Shin v'Tav.*
	Twenty-two letters and that's enough.
זְמַן לִקְרֹא, לִקְרֹא עִבְרִית.	*Z'man likro, likro Ivrit.* (2x)

TRANSLATION:
Time (3x)
Time to read Hebrew
Time (3x)
Forward!
Time to Read Hebrew.

BOKER TOV

(Good-Getting-Up-Morning Song)

Words and Music: Fran Avni

G♯m7 C♯m F♯m B7 A E
bo - ker tov ba - bo - ker om - rim Bo - ker tov Bo - ker
Instrumental
F♯m B G♯m7 C♯m F♯m7 B7
Esus E
Verse 2
E Emaj7 A/E B/E E
Ba - bo - ker ba - ki - tah ha - Mo - rah o - me - ret
A F♯m7 B E Emaj7
bo - ker tov bo - ker tov L'- tal - mid o tal - mi - dah L'-
A/E E A B E
Chorus
F♯m7 B7
chol ha - ki - tah Bo - ker bo - ker tov bo - ker tov
G♯m7 C♯m F♯m7 A/B Emaj7 E7 A B7
bo - ker tov ba - bo - ker om - rim Bo - ker tov Bo - ker tov
Repeat to fade
G♯m7 C♯m F♯m B7 A E
bo - ker tov ba - bo - ker om - rim Bo - ker tov Bo - ker

בֹּקֶר טוֹב! BOKER TOV

(GOOD-GETTING-UP-MORNING SONG)

In the morning, as we rise,
Open up our sleepy eyes,
We say, "Good Morning, *Boker Tov*" (2x)

בֹּקֶר טוֹב! (2x)

בַּבֹּקֶר, בַּבַּיִת, אִמָּא אוֹמֶרֶת:
בֹּקֶר טוֹב! (2x)
לְיֶלֶד אוֹ יַלְדָּה,
לְכָל הַמִּשְׁפָּחָה,
בֹּקֶר, בֹּקֶר טוֹב!

Ba-boker ba-bayit, Ima omeret
Boker tov (2x)
L'yeled o yaldah
L' chol ha-mishpachah.
Boker, Boker Tov.

CHORUS:

בֹּקֶר טוֹב!

Boker Tov, Boker Tov,
Ba-boker omrim Boker Tov (2x)

בַּבֹּקֶר, בַּכִּתָּה, הַמּוֹרָה אוֹמֶרֶת:
בֹּקֶר טוֹב! (2x)
לְתַלְמִיד אוֹ תַּלְמִידָה, לְכָל הַכִּתָּה,
בֹּקֶר, בֹּקֶר טוֹב!

Ba-boker ba-kitah, ha-Morah omeret
Boker Tov (2x)
L'talmid o talmidah, l'chol ha-kitah
Boker, Boker Tov.

CHORUS

TRANSLATION:
In the morning, at home, Mother says
"Good Morning"
to boy or girl, to the whole family -
"Morning - Good Morning."

CHORUS:
"Good Morning," in the morning
we say "Good Morning."

In the morning, in the classroom,
the teacher says "Good Morning"
to boy/student or girl/student
to the whole class.

CHATULIM BA-CHATUNAH

(Feline Felicity)

Words and Music: Fran Avni

Country / Bluegrass

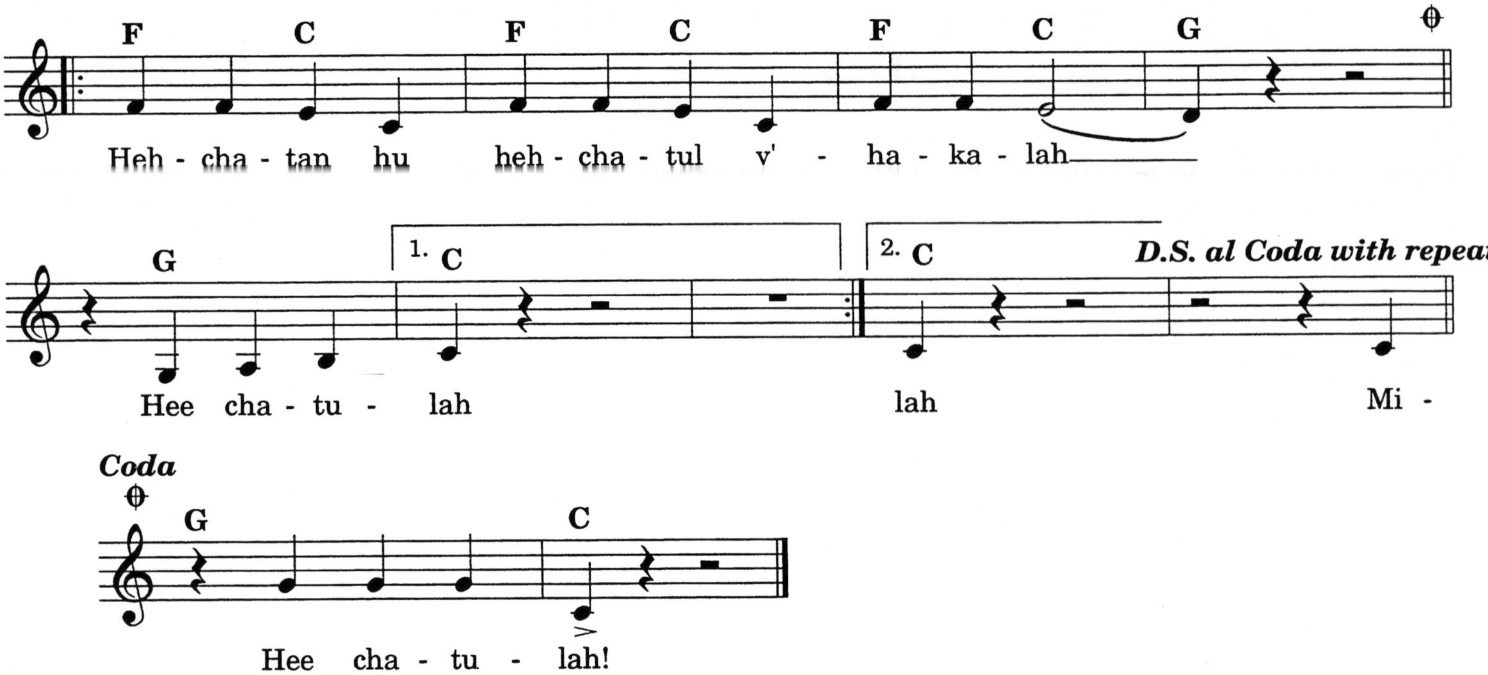
F C F C F C G
Heh - cha - tan hu heh - cha - tul v' - ha - ka - lah
G
1. C
2. C
D.S. al Coda with repeat
Hee cha - tu - lah
lah
Mi -
Coda
G C
Hee cha - tu - lah!

חֲתוּלִים בַּחֲתֻנָּה CHATULIM BA CHATUNAH

(FELINE FELICITY!)

חַ־חַ־חַ־חַ־ח	*Cha- cha- cha- cha- cha,*
	Ha,ha ha ha ha
אֵיזוֹ חֲתֻנָּה! (2x)	*Ezo chatunah* (2x)
מִתַּחַת לַחֻפָּה	*Mi-tachat la-chupah*
חָתוּל וַחֲתוּלָה,	*Chatul va-chatullah*
חָתָן וְגַם כַּלָּה,	*Chatan v'gam kallah*
שָׂשׂוֹן וְגַם שִׂמְחָה.	*Sasson v'gam simchah.*
	CHORUS:
קוֹל שָׂשׂוֹן וְקוֹל שִׂמְחָה!	*Kol sasson v'kol simchah*
עוֹמְדִים מִתַּחַת לַחֻפָּה	*Omdim mi-tachat la chupah*
חָתָן וְגַם כַּלָּה,	*Chatan v'gam kallah*
חָתוּל וַחֲתוּלָה. (2x)	*Chatul va-chatullah.* (2x)
הֶחָתָן הוּא הֶחָתוּל	*Heh-chatan hu heh-chatul*
וְהַכַּלָּה —	*V'ha-kallah -*
הִיא חֲתוּלָה. (2x)	*Hee chatullah.* (2x)
מִי בַּחֲתֻנָּה	*Mi ba-chatunah?*
מִתַּחַת לַחֻפָּה?	*Mi-tachat la-chupah?*
חָתוּל וַחֲתוּלָה,	*Chatul va-chatullah*
חָתָן וְגַם כַּלָּה.	*Chatan v'gam kallah.*
	CHORUS: 2X

TRANSLATION:
What a wedding!
Under the chupah
Cat (m) and cat (f)
Bridegroom and bride
Joy and gladness.

CHORUS:
The voice of joy, and the voice of gladness
Standing beneath the chupah
Bridegroom and bride
Cat (m) and cat (f)

The bridegroom is the "he" cat
And the bride is the "she" cat

Who is at the wedding?
Beneath the chupah?
Cat (m) and cat (f)
Bridegroom and bride.

MAZAL TOV !
(Congratulations Are in Order)

Words and Music: Fran Avni

Klezmer style - lively

Gm Cm E♭ B♭ E♭ Fm
cha - tu - nah l' - cha - tan v' - la - ka - lah Ma - zal Tov sim -
Cm G7 Cm Instrumental
chah ra - bah Ma - zal Tov la - mish - pa - chah
G Cm
Chorus
A♭ E♭
Ma - zal Tov Ma - zal Tov om -
Fm Cm Fm Cm
rim ku - lam Ma - zal Tov Ma - zal Tov sim - chah ra - bah Ma -
G7 Cm G7 D G7 Cm
zal Tov la - mish - pa - chah Ma - zal Tov la - mish - pa - chah!

מַזָּל טוֹב! MAZAL TOV!

(CONGRATULATIONS ARE IN ORDER)

VERSE 1:

הַיּוֹם לְדָנִי יֵשׁ בַּר־מִצְוָה.
מַזָּל טוֹב לַמִּשְׁפָּחָה!
הַיּוֹם לְרוּתִי יֵשׁ בַּת־מִצְוָה.
מַזָּל טוֹב לַמִּשְׁפָּחָה!

Ha-yom l'Danny yesh Bar Mitzvah.
Mazal Tov la-mishpachah.
Ha-yom l'Ruti yesh Bat Mitzvah.
Mazal Tov la-mishpachah. (2x)

CHORUS:

מַזָּל טוֹב
אוֹמְרִים כֻּלָּם: מַזָּל טוֹב
מַזָּל טוֹב, שִׂמְחָה רַבָּה!
מַזָּל טוֹב לַמִּשְׁפָּחָה! (2x)

Mazal Tov, Mazal Tov,
Omrim kulam "Mazal Tov"
Mazal Tov, Simchah Rabbah,
Mazal Tov la-mishpachah. (2x)

VERSE 2:

מַזָּל טוֹב בַּחֲתֻנָּה!
לֶחָתָן וְלַכַּלָּה.
מַזָּל טוֹב, שִׂמְחָה רַבָּה!
מַזָּל טוֹב לַמִּשְׁפָּחָה!

Mazal Tov ba-chatunah,
L'chatan v'la-kallah.
Mazal Tov, Simchah Rabbah,
Mazal Tov la-mishpachah.

CHORUS

TRANSLATION:
Today is Danny's Bar Mitzvah.
Mazal Tov to the family.
Today is Ruti's Bat Mitzvah.
Everyone says "Mazal Tov -
Mazal Tov - much joy!"

"Mazal Tov" at a wedding -
To the bridegroom and the bride.

BA-KITAH
(Classroom Capers)

Words and Music: Fran Avni

Brightly

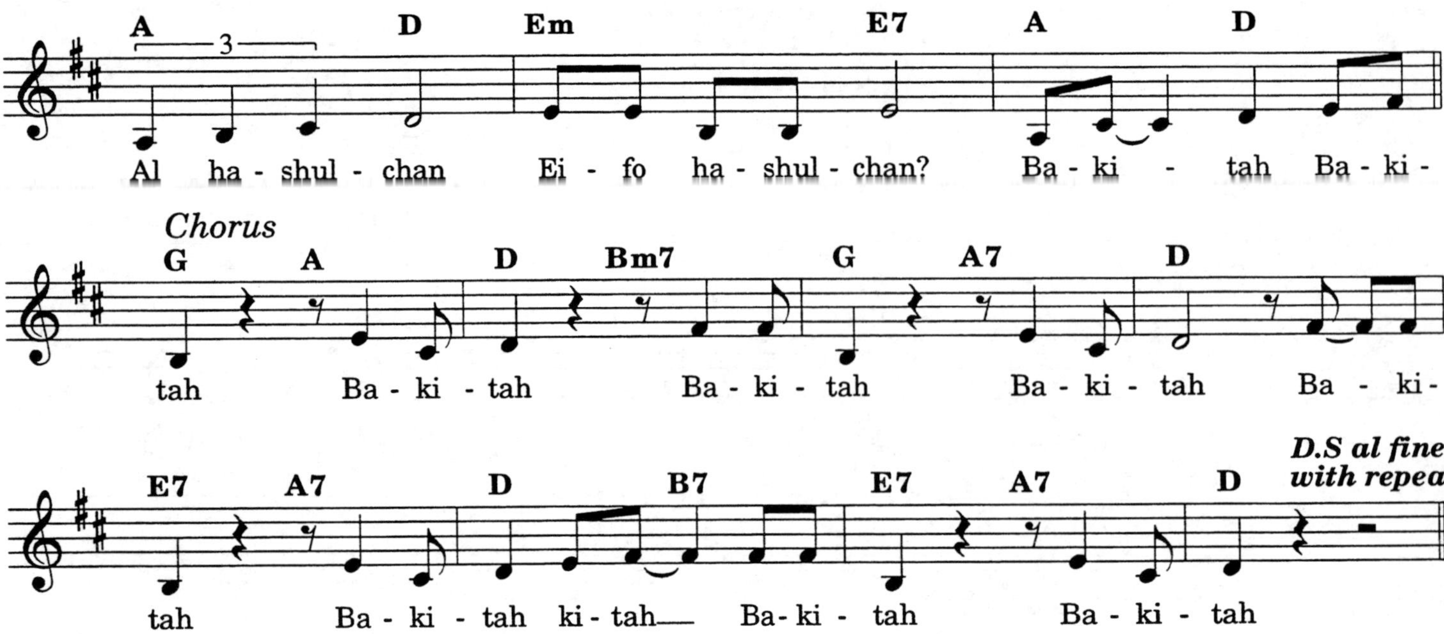

בַּכִּתָּה BA-KITAH

(CLASSROOM CAPERS)

REFRAIN:

לוּחַ וְגִיר, — *Luach v'gir*
מַחְבֶּרֶת וְעִפָּרוֹן, — *Machberet v'iparon*
שֻׁלְחָן וְכִסֵּא, — *Shulchan v'kiseh*
בַּכִּתָּה, בַּכִּתָּה. — *Ba-kitah, ba-kitah.* (3x)

VERSE 1:

אֵיפֹה הָעִפָּרוֹן? — *Eifo ha-iparon?*
עַל הַמַּחְבֶּרֶת. — *Al ha-machberet.*
אֵיפֹה הַמַּחְבֶּרֶת? — *Eifo ha-machberet?*
עַל הַכִּסֵּא. — *Al ha-kiseh.*
אֵיפֹה הַכִּסֵּא? — *Eifo ha-kiseh?*
בַּכִּתָּה — *Ba-kitah.*

CHORUS:

בַּכִּתָּה (8x) — *Ba-kitah* (8x)

VERSE 2:

אֵיפֹה הַגִּיר? — *Eifo ha-gir?*
עַל הַסֵּפֶר. — *Al ha-sefer.*
אֵיפֹה הַסֵּפֶר? — *Eifo ha-sefer?*
עַל הַשֻּׁלְחָן — *Al ha-shulchan.*
אֵיפֹה הַשֻּׁלְחָן? — *Eifo ha-shulchan?*
בַּכִּתָּה — *Ba-kitah.*

CHORUS:

בַּכִּתָּה (8x)	*Ba-kitah* (8x)

REFRAIN:

לוּחַ וְגִיר,	*Luach v'gir*
מַחְבֶּרֶת וְעִפָּרוֹן,	*Machberet v'iparon*
שֻׁלְחָן וְכִסֵּא,	*Shulchan v'kiseh*
בַּכִּתָּה, בַּכִּתָּה.	*Ba-kitah, ba-kitah.*

OPTIONAL VERSE:

אֵיפֹה הַכִּתָּה?	*Eifo ha-kitah?*
הַכִּתָּה בְּבֵית הַסֵּפֶר.	*Ha-kitah b' veit sefer.*
אֵיפֹה בֵּית הַסֵּפֶר?	*Eifo beit sefer?*
בְּבֵית כְּנֶסֶת.	*B'veit knesset.*
אֵיפֹה ... בַּעִיר, בַּמְדִינָה ...	*Eifo...ba-ir, bam' dinah,* etc.

TRANSLATION:

REFRAIN:
Chalkboard and chalk,
Notebook and pencil,
Table and chair
In the classroom.

VERSE 1:
Where is the pencil? On the notebook.
Where is the notebook? On the chair.
Where is the chair? In the classroom.

VERSE 2:
Where is the chalk? On the book.
Where is the book? On the table.
Where is the table? In the classroom.

MI LOMED IVRIT?
(Who Is Learning What?)

Words and Music: Fran Avni

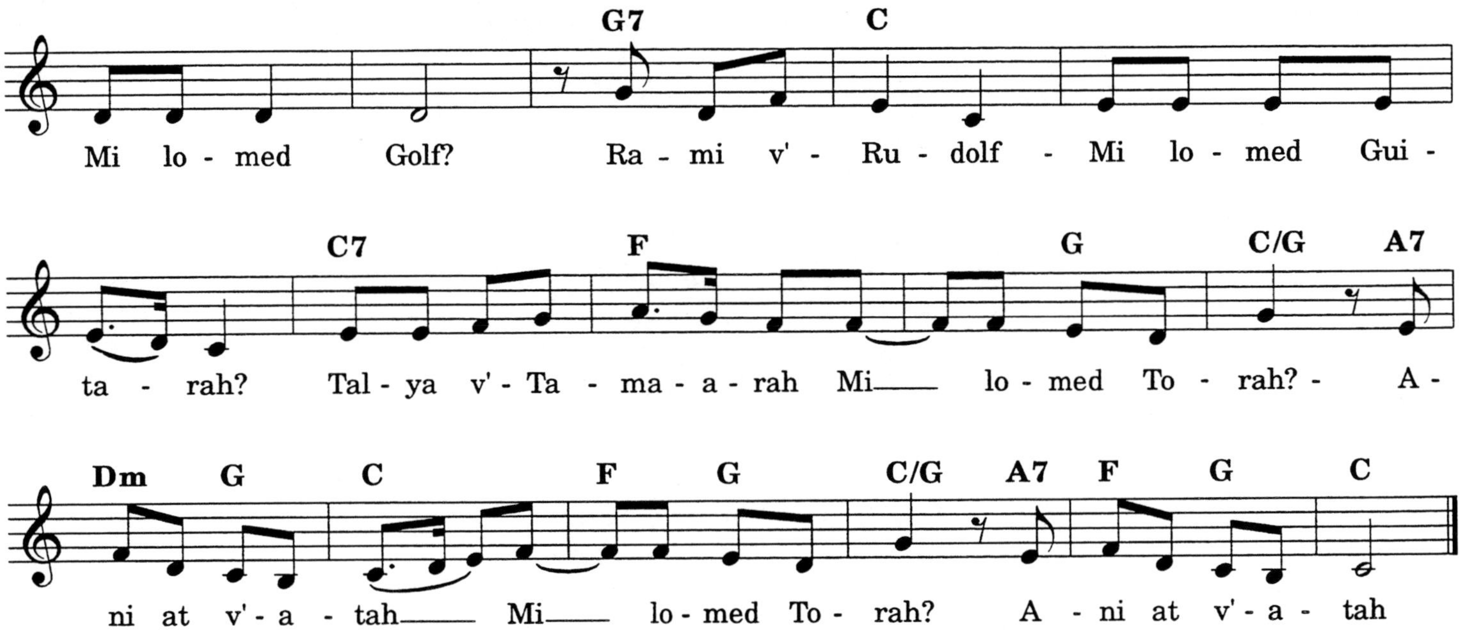
G7 C
Mi lo - med Golf? Ra - mi v' - Ru - dolf - Mi lo - med Gui -
C7 F G C/G A7
ta - rah? Tal - ya v' - Ta - ma - a - rah Mi lo - med To - rah? - A -
Dm G C F G C/G A7 F G C
ni at v' - a - tah Mi lo - med To - rah? A - ni at v' - a - tah

מִי לוֹמֵד עִבְרִית? MI LOMED IVRIT?

(WHO IS LEARNING WHAT?)

מִי לוֹמֵד עִבְרִית?	*Mi lomed Ivrit?*
—רוֹנִי וְרוֹנִית.	*- Roni v'Ronit.*
מִי לוֹמֵד טֶנִיס?	*Mi lomed tennis?*
—דָּנִי וְדֶנִיס.	*- Danny v'Dennis.*
מִי לוֹמֵד הִסְטוֹרְיָה?	*Mi lomed historiah?*
—גִּילָה וְגְלוֹרְיָה.	*- Gila v'Gloria.*
מִי לוֹמֵד תּוֹרָה?	*Mi lomed Torah?*
—אֲנִי, אַתְּ וְאַתָּה. (2x)	*- Ani, at v'atah.* (2x)
מִי לוֹמֵד בֵּיסְבּוֹל?	*Mi lomed basebol?*
—קָארִין וְקָארוֹל.	*- Kareen v'Karol.*
מִי לוֹמֵד גּוֹלְף?	*Mi lomed golf?*
—רָמִי וְרוּדוֹלְף.	*- Rami v'Rudolph.*
מִי לוֹמֵד גִּיטָארָה?	*Mi lomed guitara?*
—טַלְיָה וְתָמָרָה.	*- Taliah v'Tamarah.*
מִי לוֹמֵד תּוֹרָה?	*Mi lomed Torah?*
—אֲנִי, אַתְּ וְאַתָּה. (2x)	*- Ani, at v'atah.* (2x)
מַה לוֹמֵד דֶנִיס?	*Mah lomed Dennis?*
דֶנִיס לוֹמֵד טֶנִיס.	*Dennis lomed tennis!*
מַה לוֹמֶדֶת גְלוֹרְיָה?	*Mah lomedet Gloria?*
גְלוֹרְיָה לוֹמֶדֶת הִסְטוֹרְיָה	*Gloria lomedet historiah!*
מַה אַתָּה לוֹמֵד?	*Mah atah lomed?*
מַה אַתְּ לוֹמֶדֶת?	*Mah at lomedet?*

TRANSLATION:
Who is learning/studying Hebrew? Roni and Ronit.
Who is studying tennis? Danny and Dennis.
Who is studying history? Gila and Gloria.
Who is learning Torah? Me, you (f) and you (m).

Who is studying baseball? Kareen and Karol.
Who is learning golf? Rami and Rudolph.
Who is learning guitar? Talia and Tamarah.
Who - Torah? I, you (f) and you (m).

What is Dennis studying? Dennis is studying tennis.
What is Gloria studying? Gloria is studying history.

What are you (m) studying?
What are you (f) studying?

HIPPO BA-MAYIM

(Water Play)

Words and Music: Fran Avni

Am Em Am C E Am
A - ba ba - ma - yim ma - yim b' - sa - son
Am Em Am C D E
I - ma ba - ma - yim ma - yim ma - yim b' - sa - son
Am Em Am C E Am Em
I - ma ba - ma - yim ma - yim b' - sa - son Y' - la -
Am Em Am C D E
dim ba - ma - yim ma - yim ma - yim b' - sa - son Y' - la -
Am Em Am C E Am Em
dim ba - ma - yim ma - yim b' - sa - son Cha - tu -
Am Em Am
lim ba - ma - yim Oy! Cha - tu - lim Lo o - ha - vim ma - yim!

הִיפּוֹ בַּמַּיִם HIPPO BA-MAYIM

(WATER PLAY)

מַיִם (6x) בְּשָׂשׂוֹן. (2x)	*Mayim* (6) *B'sasson.* (2x)
הִיפּוֹ בַּמַּיִם,	*Hippo ba-mayim*
מַיִם (2x) בְּשָׂשׂוֹן.	*Mayim* (2x) *b'sasson* (2x)
הִיפּוֹ בַּמַּיִם,	*Hippo ba-mayim*
מַיִם בְּשָׂשׂוֹן.	*Mayim b'sasson,*
דָּג בַּמַּיִם,	*Dag ba-mayim*
מַיִם (2x) בְּשָׂשׂוֹן.	*Mayim* (2x) *b'sasson.*
דָּג בַּמַּיִם,	*Dag ba-mayim*
מַיִם בְּשָׂשׂוֹן.	*Mayim b'sasson.*
אַבָּא בַּמַּיִם, ...	*Abba ba-mayim.....*
אִמָּא בַּמַּיִם, ...	*Ima ba-mayim......*
יְלָדִים בַּמַּיִם, ...	*Y'ladim ba-mayim......*
חֲתוּלִים בַּמַּיִם, ...	*Chatullim ba-mayim*
מַיִם מַיִם בְּשָׂשׂוֹן	*Mayim mayim b'sasson -*
אוֹי! חֲתוּלִים לֹא אוֹהֲבִים מַיִם!	*Oy! Chatullim lo ohavim mayim!* (spoken)

TRANSLATION:
Hippo in the water -
Water, water joyfully

Fish...
Father...
Mother...
Children...
Cats...oops -
Cats do not like water!

LAILAH TOV
(Goodnight - Sleepy Time)

Words and Music: Fran Avni

Gently (Lullaby)

לַיְלָה טוֹב LAILAH TOV
(GOODNIGHT-SLEEPY TIME)

	When the stars come out to play,
	And the moon is shining bright,
לַיְלָה טוֹב!	*Lailah Tov* is what we say -
(2x) לַיְלָה טוֹב!	*Lailah Tov* - Good night - good night.
לַיְלָה טוֹב! יַלְדָּה קְטַנָּה,	*Lailah tov yaldah k'tanah,*
לַיְלָה טוֹב! יֶלֶד קָטָן.	*Lailah tov yeled katan.*
לַיְלָה טוֹב! חָתוּל וְחֲתוּלָה.	Good night *chatul va-chatullah,*
לַיְלָה טוֹב!	*Lailah tov* to everyone.
דָּג וְזֶבְּרָה, קֶנְגָּרוּ,	*Dag v'zebra, kangaroo,*
	All the creatures in the zoo,
	Sleepy in the dimming light,
לַיְלָה טוֹב!	*Lailah Tov* - good night,
	Good night!
לַיְלָה טוֹב!	*Lailah Tov!*

ANI OHEVET ET HA-CHAGIM

(I Love Holidays -"Foody Blues")

Words and Music: Fran Avni

Cm Cm/B♭ A♭ G Cm Cm/B♭
ki ba-cha-gim och-lim d'va-rim to-vim A-ni o-he-vet et ha-
F/A A♭ G Cm
cha-gim och-lim d'va-rim to-vim
Chanukah
C C/E Dm7
Ba-Cha-nu-kah Ba-Cha-nu-kah L' vi-vah cha-mah Ba-
G7 Dm7 G7 Dm7 G7 C
cha-nu-kah Ba-Cha-nu-kah l'-vi-vah cha-mah
Pesach
C C/B♭ Am Fm/A♭ C/G G7 1. C 2. C
U-v'-Pe-sach u-v'-Pe-sach rak ma-tzah tzah A-
Refrain
Cm Cm/B♭ A♭7 G Cm Cm/B♭
ni o-he-vet et ha-cha-gim ki ba-cha-gim och-lim d'va-
A♭ G Cm Cm/B♭ F/A A♭
rim to-vim A-ni o-he-vet et ha-cha-gim och-
G Cm
lim d'va-rim to-vim
Purim
C G/B Am
U-v'-Pu-rim oz-nei Ha-man

Refrain
ni o - he - vet et ha - cha - gim
Ki ba - cha - gim och - lim d'va -
rim to - vim
A - ni o - he - vet et ha - cha - gim
och -
lim d'va - rim to - vim
A -
A - val b' -
Yom Ki - pur
Lo och - lim!

אֲנִי אוֹהֶבֶת אֶת הַחַגִּים ANI OHEVET ET HA-CHAGIM

(I LOVE HOLIDAYS - "FOODY BLUES")

	REFRAIN:
אֲנִי אוֹהֶבֶת אֶת הַחַגִּים	*Ani ohevet et ha-chagim*
כִּי בַּחַגִּים אוֹכְלִים דְּבָרִים	*Ki ba-chagim ochlim d'varim*
טוֹבִים. (2x)	*tovim.* (2x)
תַּפּוּחִים בִּדְבַשׁ	*Tapuchim bi- d'vash*
בְּרֹאשׁ הַשָּׁנָה ... (2x)	*B' Rosh Ha-Shanah.* (2x)
בְּשַׁבָּת, בְּשַׁבָּת	*B'Shabbat, b'Shabbat*
בְּשַׁבָּת אוֹכְלִים חַלָּה ...	*B'Shabbat ochlim challah.*
	Ani ohevet…
בַּחֲנֻכָּה, בַּחֲנֻכָּה	*Ba-Chanukah, ba-Chanukah,*
לְבִיבָה חַמָּה ... (2x)	*l'vivah chamah* (2x)
וּבְפֶסַח, וּבְפֶסַח	*U-v'Pesach, u-v'Pesach*
רַק מַצָּה! ...	*rak matzah.* (2x)
	Ani ohevet…
וּבְפּוּרִים אָזְנֵי הָמָן,	*U- v'Purim oznei Haman*
כָּל הַזְּמַן! ... (2x)	*kol ha-z'man.* (2x)
	Ani ohevet…
אֲבָל בְּיוֹם כִּפּוּר — לֹא אוֹכְלִים!	*Aval b'Yom Kippur - lo ochlim!* (spoken)

TRANSLATION:
I love the holidays,
'cause on the holidays
we eat wonderful things.
Apples and honey on Rosh HaShanah,
And on Shabbat we eat challah.
On Chanukah, hot latkes,
And on Pesach, only matzah.
On Purim, hamentashen,
But on Yom Kippur - we do not eat!

SHABBAT SHALOM
(Ready for Shabbat)

Words and Music: Fran Avni

Lyrically - Waltz

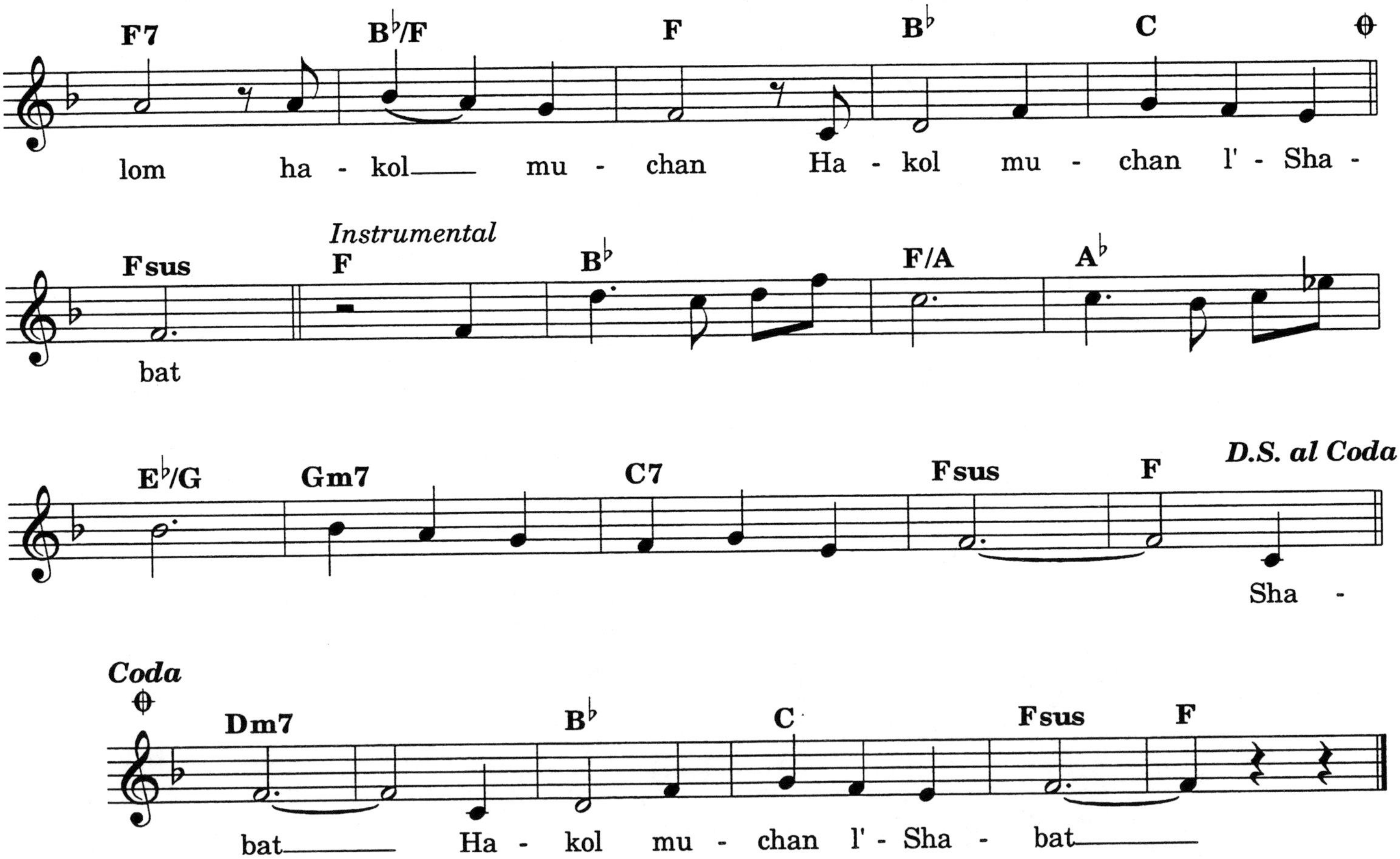

שַׁבַּת שָׁלוֹם! SHABBAT SHALOM
(READY FOR SHABBAT)

שַׁבַּת שָׁלוֹם! אִמָּא וְאַבָּא, סַבָּא, סַבְתָּא, בֵּן, גַּם בַּת. שַׁבַּת שָׁלוֹם, שַׁבַּת שָׁלוֹם, לְכָל הַמִּשְׁפָּחָה.	*Shabbat shalom Ima v'Abba, Saba, Savta, ben gam bat. Shabbat shalom, shabbat shalom, l'chol ha-mishpachah.*
מַפָּה לְבָנָה עַל הַשֻּׁלְחָן. נֵרוֹת, חַלָּה, דָּג וְיַיִן.	*Mappah l'vanah, al ha-shulchan, Nerot, challah, dag v'yayin.*
שַׁבַּת שָׁלוֹם, הַכֹּל מֻכָן הַכֹּל מֻכָן לְשַׁבָּת.	*Shabbat shalom, ha-kol muchan, Ha-kol muchan l'Shabbat.*

TRANSLATION:
Shabbat Shalom Mother, and Father,
Grandfather, Grandmother,
Son and Daughter.
Shabbat Shalom to all the Family.

White cloth on the table.
Candles, Challah,
Fish and wine.
Shabbat Shalom.
Everything's ready for Shabbat.

CHAG SAMEACH !
(Happy Holidays)

Words and Music: Fran Avni

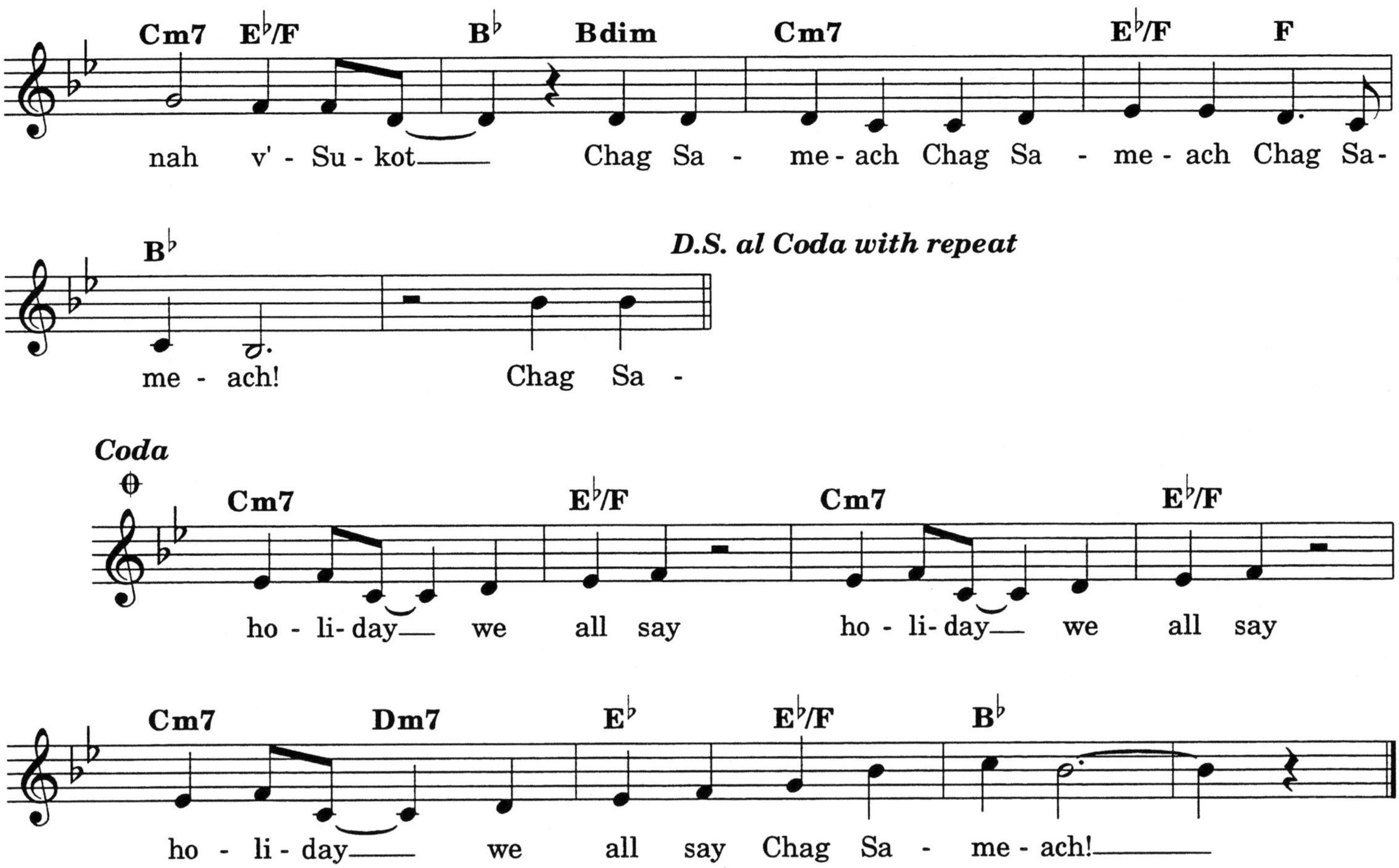

חַג שָׂמֵחַ! CHAG SAMEACH!

(HAPPY HOLIDAYS)

	CHORUS:
חַג שָׂמֵחַ לְכֻלָּם!	*Chag sameach l'chulam.*
חַג שָׂמֵחַ	*Chag sameach everyone*
	Every holiday we all say -
חַג שָׂמֵחַ!	*"Chag Sameach!"* (2x)
רֹאשׁ הַשָּׁנָה וְסֻכּוֹת,	*Rosh HaShanah v'Sukkot*
שִׂמְחַת תּוֹרָה וַחֲנֻכָּה,	*Simchat Torah va-Chanukah*
בְּפוּרִים תָּמִיד אוֹמְרִים	*B'Purim tamid omrim -*
חַג שָׂמֵחַ!	*"Chag Sameach!"*
גַּם בְּפֶסַח, שָׁבוּעוֹת,	*Gam b'Pesach, Shavuot,*
רֹאשׁ הַשָּׁנָה וְסֻכּוֹת ...	*Rosh HaShanah v'Sukkot....*
חַג שָׂמֵחַ!	*Chag Sameach* (3x)

TRANSLATION:
Happy holiday to everyone.
On Rosh HaShanah ... Chanukah,
On Purim we all say, "Happy Holiday."

LO KOL YOM PURIM
(Purim Comes but Once a Year)

Words: Dina Maiben
Music: Fran Avni

Verse 2
D E♭dim A/E A A7
Pu - rim b' - veit ha - Kne - set Ha - Cha - zan
D D7 G
ko - reh ba - me - gi - lah Mah yesh l' chol ha -
D Dm/C B7 E7 A D Am/C
ye - la - dim? rash - rash - rash Ra' - a - sha - nim.
B7 E7 A7 D D/E
Rash - rash - rash Ra - a - sha - nim
Verse 3
F♯7
Sha -
Bm F♯7/C♯ F♯ Em/C♯
bat b' - veit ha - Kne - set Ha - Ra - bi
F♯7 Bm B7 Em Em6
o - med al ha - bi - mah Mah yesh la -
Bm Bm/F♯ F♯/C♯ F♯7 Bm
Ra - bi? Ta - lit v' - ki - pah
B7 Em Em/G Bm Bm/F♯
Mah yesh la - Ra - bi Ta -

F#/C# F#7 Bm A7 Verse 4 D
lit v' li pah Sha - bat
Em/D A rit.
b' - veit ha - Kne - set Ku - lam mit - pa - le -
a Tempo rit.
D Dmaj7 D7 G D Am6/C
lim Ein ma - se - chah la - Ra
a Tempo
B7 E7 A7 D C7 B7
bi Ki lo kol yom Pu - rim
E7 A E7 A13 E7
lo kol yom lo kol yom lo kol
A13 D D/C G/B B♭ A7 D A13 D
yom Pu - rim Pu - rim!

לֹא כָּל יוֹם פּוּרִים! LO KOL YOM PURIM
(PURIM COMES BUT ONCE A YEAR!)

פּוּרִים בְּבֵית הַכְּנֶסֶת,
הָרַבִּי עוֹמֵד עַל הַבִּימָה.
מַה יֵּשׁ לָרַבִּי?
יֵשׁ—מַסֵּכָה. (2x)

Purim b'veit ha-Knesset
Ha-Rabbi omed al ha-bimah
Mah yesh la-Rabbi?
Yesh - masechah. (2x)

פּוּרִים בְּבֵית הַכְּנֶסֶת,
הַחַזָּן קוֹרֵא בַּמְּגִילָּה.
מַה יֵּשׁ לְכָל הַיְלָדִים ?
רַשׁ—רַשׁ—רַשׁ—רַעֲשָׁנִים.

Purim b'veit ha-knesset
Ha-Chazan koreh ba-megillah.
Mah yesh l'chol ha-yeladim?
Rash - rash - rash- Ra'ashanim.

שַׁבָּת בְּבֵית הַכְּנֶסֶת,
הָרַבִּי עוֹמֵד עַל הַבִּימָה.
מַה יֵּשׁ לָרַבִּי?
טַלִּית וְכִפָּה. (2x)

Shabbat b'veit ha-Knesset
Ha-Rabbi omed al ha-bimah.
Mah yesh la-Rabbi?
Tallit v'kippah. (2x)

שַׁבָּת בְּבֵית הַכְּנֶסֶת,
כֻּלָּם מִתְפַּלְלִים.
אֵין מַסֵּכָה לָרַבִּי—
כִּי לֹא כָּל יוֹם פּוּרִים!
לֹא כָּל יוֹם, לֹא כָּל יוֹם,
לֹא כָּל יוֹם פּוּרִים!

Shabbat b'veit ha-Knesset
Kulam mitpallelim.
Ein masecha la-Rabbi -
Ki lo kol yom Purim.
Lo kol yom, lo kol yom,
Lo kol yom Purim!

TRANSLATION:
Purim in the synagogue -
The Rabbi stands on the pulpit
What does the Rabbi have ?
A mask.

Purim in the synagogue -
The Cantor reads the megillah.
What do all the children have?
Gragers. (noisemakers)

Shabbat in the synagogue -
The Rabbi stands on the pulpit.
What does the Rabbi have?
A tallis and kippah.

Shabbat in the synagogue -
Everyone is praying.
The Rabbi has no mask
'Cause not every day is Purim!

MI B'SEDER PESACH?
(Four New Questions for the Seder)

Words and Music: Fran Avni

A6 A A B♭dim Bm E
der— Pe - sach? Ya - yin l'- ki - dush v'- Ha - ga - dah Ma -
Bm E Bm7 E7 D A
tzah ma - ror kar - pas cha - ro - set Gam z'- ro - a v'- gam
E A A Bm/A A Bm/A
— be - tzah Mi u - mah— Ei - fo - ha—
D C♯m7
Q.3 Mi b'- se - der Pe - sach sho - el— Mah Nish - ta - nah? Ye - led ka - tan— v'- yal - dah—
C♯m7/F♯ F♯7 Dmaj7 B7/D♯
— k'- ta - nah Mi b'- se - der Pe - sach sho - el— Mah Nish - ta - nah?
A/E F♯m Bm7 D/E A A Bm/A
Ye - led ka - tan— v'- yal - dah— k' - ta - nah
Refrain
A Bm/A A Bm/A A Bm/A
Mi b'- se - der Pe - sach?— Mah al ha - shul - chan Mi sho -
A C♯m7 Bm7 C♯m7 Dmaj7 D/E A Bm/A
el Mah Nish - ta - nah? v'- Ei - fo— ha - a - fi - ko - man?—

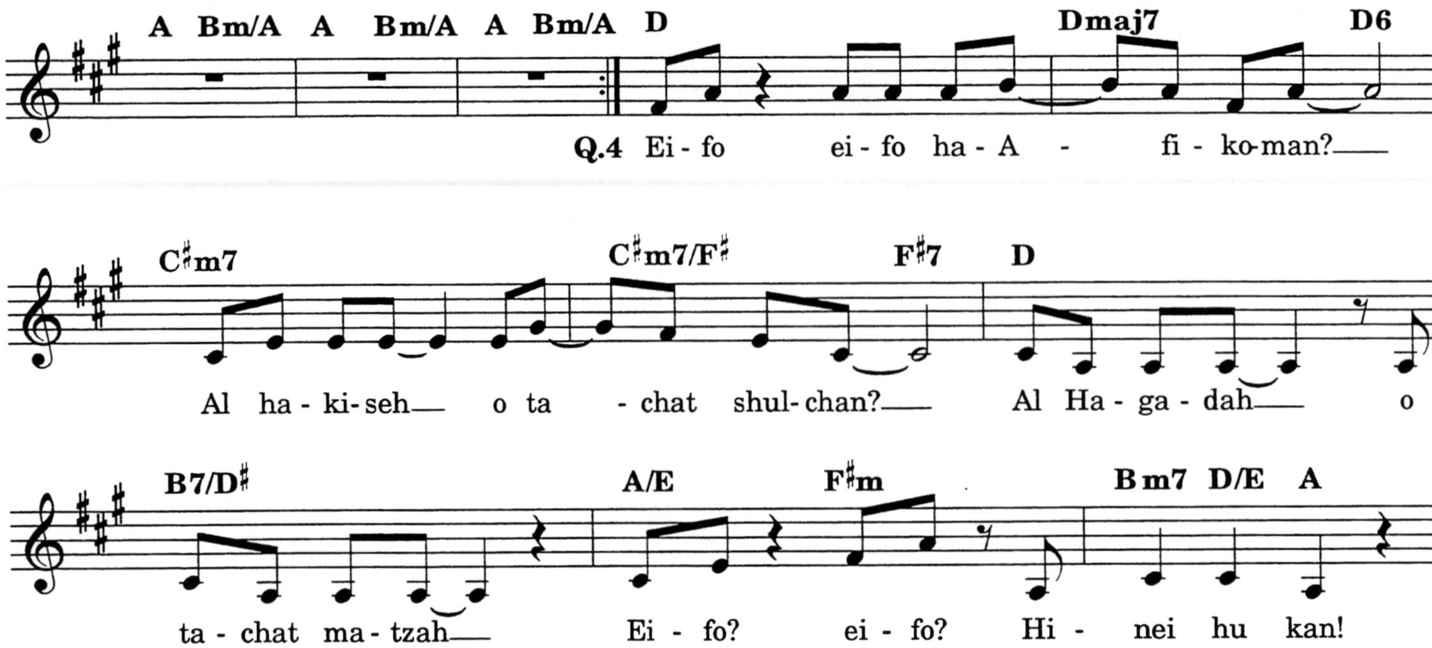

מִי בְּסֵדֶר פֶּסַח? MI B'SEDER PESACH?

(FOUR NEW QUESTIONS FOR THE SEDER)

מִי וּמַה? אֵיפֹה הַ...?	*Mi? u-Mah? Eifo ha?* (4x)
	REFRAIN:
מִי בְּסֵדֶר פֶּסַח?	*Mi b'seder Pesach?*
מָה עַל הַשֻּׁלְחָן?	*Mah al ha-shulchan?*
מִי שׁוֹאֵל "מַה נִּשְׁתַּנָּה"?	*Mi shoel "Mah Nishtanah?"*
וְאֵיפֹה הָאֲפִיקוֹמָן? (2x)	*V'eifo ha-Afikoman?* (2x)
	QUESTION 1
מִי בְּסֵדֶר פֶּסַח?	*Mi b'seder Pesach?*
אַבָּא וְאִמָּא,	*Abba v'Ima,*
סַבָּא וְסַבְתָּא,	*Saba v'Savta*
יֶלֶד וְיַלְדָּה.	*Yeled v'yaldah*
מִי בְּסֵדֶר פֶּסַח? (3x)	*Mi b'seder Pesach?* (3x)
כָּל הַמִּשְׁפָּחָה.	*Kol ha-mishpachah.*
	QUESTION 2:
מָה עַל הַשֻּׁלְחָן בְּסֵדֶר פֶּסַח?	*Mah al ha-shulchan b'seder Pesach?*
יַיִן לְקִדּוּשׁ וְהַגָּדָה,	*Yayin l'kiddush v'Haggadah,*
מַצָּה, מָרוֹר, כַּרְפַּס, חֲרוֹסֶת,	*Matzah, maror, karpas, charoset,*
גַּם זְרוֹעַ וְגַם בֵּיצָה.	*Gam z'roa v'gam betzah.*

מִי וּמַה? אֵיפֹה הַ...?

CHORUS: *Mi, Mah, Eifo ha?*

QUESTION 3:

מִי בְּסֵדֶר פֶּסַח
שׁוֹאֵל "מַה נִּשְׁתַּנָּה"?
יֶלֶד קָטָן וְיַלְדָּה קְטַנָּה.

Mi b'seder Pesach
Shoel "Mah Nishtanah?"
Yeled katan v'yaldah k'tanah. (2x)

REFRAIN:

מִי בְּסֵדֶר פֶּסַח?
מָה עַל הַשֻּׁלְחָן?
מִי שׁוֹאֵל "מַה נִּשְׁתַּנָּה"?
וְאֵיפֹה הָאֲפִיקוֹמָן?

Mi b'seder Pesach?
Mah al ha-shulchan?
Mi shoel "Mah Nishtanah?"
V' eifo ha-afikoman?

QUESTION 4:

אֵיפֹה, אֵיפֹה הָאֲפִיקוֹמָן?
עַל הַכִּסֵּא, אוֹ תַּחַת שֻׁלְחָן?
עַל הַגָּדָה, אוֹ תַּחַת מַצָּה?
אֵיפֹה, אֵיפֹה
הִנֵּה הוּא כָּאן!

Eifo, eifo ha-afikoman?
Al ha-kisai o tachat shulchan?
Al haggadah o tachat matzah?
Eifo, eifo?
Hinei hu kan!

TRANSLATION:
Who? What? Where?

Q.1 Who's at the Pesach seder?
A. Father, Mother, Grandpa, Grandma, boy and girl, the whole family.

Q.2 What's on the table?
A. Wine for the kiddush, haggadah, matzah, maror, karpas, charoset, as well as z'roa and betzah.

Q.3 Who asks the "Mah Nishtanah"?
A. A young boy or girl.

Q.4 Where is the Afikoman? (on the chair, or under the table - on the haggadah or under the matzah?)
A. Here it is!

SHALOM SHALOM
(Hello, Goodbye)

Words and Music: Fran Avni

שָׁלוֹם! שָׁל־ל־לוֹם! SHALOM, SHALOM
(HELLO, GOODBYE)

גַּם בַּלַּיְלָה, גַּם בַּיּוֹם,
בַּחוּץ, בִּפְנִים, בְּכָל מָקוֹם.
תָּמִיד אוֹמְרִים שָׁלוֹם, שָׁלוֹם.
תָּמִיד אוֹמְרִים שָׁלוֹם. (5x)

CHORUS:
Gam ba-lailah, gam ba-yom,
Bachutz, bifnim, b'chol makom,
Tamid omrim "Shalom, shalom".
Tamid omrim "Shalom."

Going in, going out, coming home,
Hello, goodbye, peace to everyone
Going in, going out, coming home,
We say "Shalom, shalom".

CHORUS

USING Z'MAN LASHIR IN THE CLASSROOM

The songs on the *Z'man LaShir* cassette tape can be an integral part of any Hebrew language program. They specifically reinforce the vocabulary of *Kadimah!* and *Z'man Likro*, the Hebrew decoding program also published by A.R.E. Publishing. *Z'man LaShir* is designed to introduce a core basic vocabulary in small incremental steps, with much of the vocabulary repeated and reinforced in several songs.

Teaching foreign language vocabulary through music has been found to be a powerful learning tool. Rhythm and melody enhance retention and enjoyment, and the lyrics provide opportunities to act out situations and concretize abstract concepts. Repetitive spoken drill and practice are necessary parts of learning a second language. Repeating words in song is an enjoyable way of accomplishing the same goal. Students who may be reticent to speak Hebrew words will often feel much more comfortable about singing them in a song.

Theories of language acquisition indicate that the manner of learning a second language should be similar to the way one acquires a first language: oral language preceding written language. Furthermore, receptive language should precede expressive language. This is how children acquire language — comprehension comes before speech, and speech comes before reading and writing.

In using *Z'man LaShir*, students are provided with the opportunity to acquire an oral language base (albeit a limited one) before they are confronted with print. Teachers can begin teaching the songs before students are taught any of the Hebrew letters.

It is advisable to work on developing comprehension of the vocabulary before expecting students to use it actively. Before having students join in a song, allow them time just to listen to the tape.

When you are actually ready to teach the songs, the enthusiasm you project is much more important than the musical talents either you or your students possess. Rely on the tape to learn and teach the melodies. If you play an instrument you can later accompany yourself and your students. If your students can already read Hebrew, distribute song sheets or use an overhead projector to show the words to the songs.

Following are several guidelines for teaching the *Z'man LaShir* songs:

1. Pre-teach the most essential vocabulary needed to understand the song, especially any words in the songs that are taught in *Kadimah!* and *Z'man Likro*.

2. Some of the *Z'man LaShir* vocabulary is reinforced only in *Z'man Likro*. If possible, teach these songs before you teach those words in *Z'man Likro*. In this way the vocabulary will be familiar and already part of the Hebrew oral language. The chart on page 53 summarizes the type of vocabulary taught in *Z'man LaShir* organized according to language function.

3. Use body movement, hand motions, puppets, pictures, and/or actual objects to act out the meaning of different words and phrases.

4. It is not essential to teach all of the vocabulary in the songs. Some of the more conceptual phrases (such as "everything's ready") can be quickly translated as you are singing the songs and don't need to be specifically taught. Don't worry about students understanding each and every word of a song, as long as they understand the important words and the basic theme.

5. Once students have mastered a song, provide them with rhythm instruments and encourage them to use these as they sing.

Following are specific recommendations for teaching each of the songs on *Z'man LaShir* along with the Unit and/or Lesson relevant for each song in both *Kadimah!* and *Z'man Likro*.

SIDE A

1. "Time To Read Hebrew"/"זְמַן לִקְרֹא": *Kadimah!*, Unit 6; *Z'man Likro*, Lessons 14 and/or 18.

   This is an Aleph Bet song that teaches the names of the letters of the Hebrew alphabet in order, omitting the letters ב, כ, פ, שׂ which are not taught in *Kadimah!*. If you have a Hebrew letter chart that excludes these (and the final letters), point to the letters as you sing the song. The melody is very similar to the one used in the well-known ABC song. The title of both *Kadimah!* and *Z'man Likro* are mentioned in the song. Explain to students that קָדִימָה means "Forward!" and that זְמַן לִקְרֹא means "Time To Read." Note the ticking clock sound in the background which reinforces the meaning of *"z'man"* (time).

2. "Good-Getting-Up-Morning Song"/ "בֹּקֶר טוֹב": *Z'man Likro*, Lesson 13.

   This song has an upbeat, morning feel to it. Use pictures to illustrate the important words in the song: יֶלֶד קָטָן, יַלְדָּה קְטַנָּה. If your students already have acquired other vocabulary you can substitute אִמָּא עוֹמֶדֶת with אַבָּא אוֹמֵר.

   Explain the difference between הַמּוֹרֶה אוֹמֵר and הַמּוֹרָה אוֹמֶרֶת.

3. "Feline Felicity"/ "חֲתוּלִים בַּחֲתֻנָּה": *Kadimah!*, Lesson 9; *Z'man Likro*, Lesson 8.

   Have fun with this one. The concept of a wedding of two cats is quite comical. If you are teaching the song in conjunction with *Kadimah!*, students will just be learning the Chet sound. It is probably the most difficult of Hebrew sounds to pronounce, so the song is quite challenging to sing. The sound is repeated often — beginning with the laughing חָה, חָה, חָה, חָה to the repetition of חָתוּל וַחֲתוּלָה מִתַּחַת לַחֻפָּה. Show students pictures of חֲתֻנָּה, חֻפָּה, חֲתוּלָה, and חָתוּל and name them.

   Distribute cut out magazine photos of two cats to each student, and have them paste these onto a piece of paper and dress them up as חָתָן and כַּלָּה using crayons and/or markers. Help students distinguish between the words חָתוּל and חָתָן; חֲתוּלָה and כַּלָּה. When they complete this, have them draw a chupah above the cats. You can also have volunteers act out the "cats' wedding," using a tallit for the chupah and masks for the cats.

   Use hand signs to illustrate the verb עוֹמְדִים. You can play a game *Simon Says* if you also teach יוֹשְׁבִים/יוֹשֵׁב. If students have not been introduced to verbs yet, you do not need to explain that עוֹמְדִים is in plural form. Note, however, that עוֹמֵד is used in the Purim song, "*Lo Kol Yom Purim.*"

4. "Congratulations are in Order"/"מַזָּל טוֹב": *Z'man Likro*, Lesson 14).

   Discuss the different occasions on which we would wish someone Mazal Tov. Use pictures to illustrate the occasions mentioned in the song (Bar Mitzvah, Bat Mitzvah, wedding). Make sure students are pronouncing the expression as it is said in Hebrew, מַזָּל טוֹב (accent on *"zal"*) rather than the Yiddish Mazel Tov. Teach the vocabulary קוֹל שָׂשׂוֹן. Since it appears in several of the songs in *Z'man LaShir*.

VOCABULARY IN Z'MAN LASHIR

Greetings	Animals	Jewish Ritual	Jewish Celebrations			
			Life Cycle	Purim	Pesach	Shabbat
שָׁלוֹם בֹּקֶר טוֹב לַיְלָה טוֹב מַזָּל טוֹב חַג שָׂמֵחַ	דָּג (בַּמַּיִם) חָתוּל/חֲתוּלָה חֲתוּלִים זֶבְּרָה קֶנְגוּרוּ הִיפּוֹ	בֵּית כְּנֶסֶת רַבִּי חַזָּן בִּימָה כִּפָּה טַלִּית	חֲתֻנָּה חָתָן כַּלָּה חוּפָּה קוֹל שָׂשׂוֹן קוֹל שִׂמְחָה בַּר מִצְוָה בַּת מִצְוָה	מַסֵּכָה מְגִילָּה רַעֲשָׁנִים	סֵדֶר הַגָּדָה מַצָּה מָרוֹר, כַּרְפַּס חֲרוֹסֶת זְרוֹעַ בֵּיצָה מַה נִּשְׁתַּנָּה	מַפָּה (לְבָנָה) נֵרוֹת חַלָּה דָּג יַיִן קִדּוּשׁ

Classroom	Question Words	Adjectives	Prepositions, Adverbs	Verbs	Pronouns	Family/People
(בַּ)כִּתָּה תַּלְמִיד תַּלְמִידָה מוֹרָה לוּחַ גִּיר מַחְבֶּרֶת עִפָּרוֹן שֻׁלְחָן כִּסֵּא סֵפֶר	מִי מַה אֵיפֹה (אֵיזוֹ)	קָטָן, קְטַנָּה לְבָנָה טוֹבִים	עַל מִ (תַּחַת) וְ־ בְּ־ כְּ־ הַ־ כָּל, הַכֹּל לְכֹל, כֻּלָּם לֹא	לוֹמֵד, לוֹמֶדֶת אוֹהֵב, אוֹהֶבֶת אוֹהֲבִים עוֹמֵד, עוֹמֶדֶת עוֹמְדִים אוֹמֵר, אוֹמֶרֶת אוֹמְרִים שׁוֹאֵל, שׁוֹאֶלֶת אוֹכֵל, אוֹכֶלֶת אוֹכְלִים מִתְפַּלְלִים קוֹרֵא, לִקְרֹא יֵשׁ, אֵין	אֲנִי אַתָּה אַתְּ (הִיא)	אִמָּא, אַבָּא סַבָּא, סַבְתָּא בֵּן, בַּת יֶלֶד, יַלְדָּה

5. "Classroom Capers"/"בַּכִּתָּה":
Kadimah!, Unit 2; *Z'man Likro*, Lesson 10.

This song was designed to teach classroom words, the question word אֵיפֹה (where) and two prepositions: עַל and בְּ־.

The objects mentioned in the song are: chalkboard לוּחַ, chalk גִּיר, notebook מַחְבֶּרֶת, pencil עִפָּרוֹן, table שֻׁלְחָן, chair כִּסֵּא, book סֵפֶר.

This vocabulary lends itself to acting out. Demonstrate the word בַּכִּתָּה by making a sweeping motion to encompass the entire room. Translate if needed. Teach the classroom vocabulary by pointing to the objects. For example, point to a pencil and say עִפָּרוֹן, then point to a book and say סֵפֶר. Repeat several times until all students can point to the new words.

When these two nouns are mastered, demonstrate (one at a time) the prepositions עַל and תַּחַת. Teach all of the vocabulary before you sing the song. As you sing, have students point to the objects in the refrain: לוח וגיר/מחברת ועפרון/שלחן וכסא. This technique can be used with other songs as well. When you are singing the verses, have students hold up their hands in a questioning position as they ask each question. As you sing the responses act them out. When students have mastered the vocabulary sing the song slowly and ask students to act out the responses. Make sure that they have all the objects needed.

6. "Who is Learning What?"/
"מִי לוֹמֵד עִבְרִית": *Z'man Likro*, Lesson 13.

This song directly drills the singular masculine form of the verb לוֹמֵד. The subjects being studied are mostly cognates, i.e., English words used in Hebrew, but some of these are pronounced slightly differently in Hebrew. Pay attention to the pronunciation. Ask students to guess what the "subjects" are: טֶנִיס, גּוֹלְף, בֵּיס־בּוֹל, הִסְטוֹרְיָה. Students will be amused by this, and you may wish to have them guess other words that are not used in the song (for example, גֵּאוֹגְרַפְיָה, בִּיוֹלוֹגְיָה).

Prepare pictures (or objects) that illustrate what each child in the song is learning, and corresponding English and/or Hebrew name cards for each of the children in the song. Pass out the name cards to individual students. Display the pictures or objects illustrating what each child in the song is learning. Redistribute the name cards and sing the song again. After students have heard the song several times play various games that require them to respond to each of the questions either by singing the response or demonstrating it with a picture or movement.

Explain that we ask "Who learns עִבְרִית?" in the masculine singular form, since we do not know if the answer is going to be singular or plural, masculine or feminine. But, in the final lines of the song, when the question asks what each specific child is learning, we do know which child the question is asking about, so we do use לוֹמֵד for a boy and לוֹמֶדֶת for a girl.

When you sing the line containing the words אֲנִי, אַתְּ, וְאַתָּה, point to yourself, to a girl at whom you look, and to a boy at whom you look. Practice the verb in the masculine (לוֹמֵד) and feminine (לוֹמֶדֶת) form using students in the classroom and/or puppets.

a. Point to a child and ask the students if you say לוֹמֵד or לוֹמֶדֶת.

b. After students can do this reliably, have them say a complete sentence together: (דָּנִי) לוֹמֵד עִבְרִית.

Initially use one subject (e.g., דָּנִי) and then alternate by using the pictures and/or objects you used to teach the song. Other regular verbs used in *Z'man LaShir* are: אוֹהֵב (love/like), אוֹמֵר (say), שׁוֹאֵל (ask), and עוֹמֵד (stand). Notice that the verbs לוֹמֵד and עוֹמֵד sound much alike and can easily get confused. Do not teach these together.

7. "Water Play"/"הַיָּפוֹ בַּמַּיִם": *Kadimah!*, Unit 3: *Z'man Likro*, Lessons 7 and 8.

In addition to the names of animals the song teaches the word בַּמַּיִם and the plural masculine form of love/like אוֹהֲבִים.

The song lends itself to acting out, using costume pieces or puppets. Note that each character has an accompanying sound on the tape, from the whistling of the children to the tinkling sound of the fish.

8. "Good Night—Sleepy Time"/"לַיְלָה טוֹב": *Kadimah!*, Unit 3; *Z'man Likro*, Lesson 14).

This song has both Hebrew and English text. The major phrase לַיְלָה טוֹב is translated. This song features the changing of adjectives (קָטָן or קְטַנָּה) to match the nouns (יֶלֶד or יַלְדָּה). This concept is also reinforced in the Pesach song "*Mi B'Seder Pesach*?" In *Z'man Likro*, the masculine form of big (גָּדוֹל) and small (קָטָן) are taught. The animals in the song all appear in *Kadimah!*, and except for (חָתוּל(ים are all cognates.

The mood of the song is that of a lullaby. Choose students to play the parts of the characters in the song using props or puppets and act out falling asleep. You can contrast this song with "*Boker Tov*," and its peppy, lively rhythm.

SIDE B

1. "I Love Holidays — Foody Blues"/ "אֲנִי אוֹהֶבֶת אֶת הַחַגִּים": *Z'man Likro*, Lesson 15.

This song uses the verb אוֹהֵב and reviews the different foods we eat (or don't eat!) on the Jewish holidays. Have pictures of the foods or, even better, samples of the foods available. Point to each food as you sing the song.

The song is sung in feminine singular on the cassette tape because the singer is a woman. Once they know the song, the students can change the form of the verb. Take turns having boys sing "אוֹהֵב" and girls sing "אוֹהֶבֶת." Tell them that the word אֶת is just a connecting word without meaning, not to be confused with the feminine verb ending □ת.

Note that the melody changes for each different holiday. This does make the song harder to learn initially. However, the melody changes can enhance the learning experience if students are asked to identify the original holiday melody.

2. "Ready for Shabbat"/"שַׁבָּת שָׁלוֹם": *Kadimah!*, Unit 1; *Z'man Likro*, Lesson 1.

This is a beautiful song with which to begin any child's study of Hebrew! Have a photograph or picture of an extended family on hand or ask students to bring in photographs of their parents, grandparents, and siblings. As you sing the song with your students, point to the different family members mentioned in the song, and use a sweeping motion to explain כָּל הַמִּשְׁפָּחָה. Explain the meaning of the phrase הַכֹּל מוּכָן.

In your classroom, set a Shabbat table using a white tablecloth. Demonstrate the meaning of the preposition עַל by placing different Shabbat objects on your table as the song is sung. Show students the movement used while kindling the lights of Shabbat and say the appropriate blessing.

After you have sung the song several times, have students point to pictures of different family members and the Shabbat objects as you sing the song slowly. Pick volunteers to place the Shabbat objects on the table as they are mentioned in the song.

3. "Happy Holidays"/"חַג שָׂמֵחַ": *Kadimah!*, Unit 5; *Z'man Likro*, Lesson 14.

While the vocabulary of this song is mainly taught in *Z'man Likro*, it is related to Jewish celebrations, which are also introduced in *Kadimah!*.

To demonstrate the meaning of the expression חַג שָׂמֵחַ, create a poster that illustrates the different holiday celebrations mentioned in the song. Note that the holidays are named in correct chronological order. Thus, once the words of the song are memorized, students will have learned the correct order of the major holidays. Point to each holiday picture as the song mentions it.

4. "Purim Comes but Once a Year"/ "לֹא כָּל יוֹם פּוּרִים": *Kadimah!*, Unit 5; *Z'man Likro*, Lesson 16.

This song presents a delightful contrast between the playful spirit of Purim and the more serious feeling of Shabbat. Begin your presentation with a discussion about Purim and its major symbols: the Megillah, noisemakers, masks, and costumes. Bring in props to dress up a student as the Rabbi with a mask on and another as the Cantor reading from the Megillah. Give the remaining students noisemakers. Have the students act out the words of the song as the tape is played (or as you sing the song). Specific words to act out are: מִתְפַּלְלִים, קוֹרֵא, מַסֵּכָה, עוֹמֵד, כִּפָּה, טַלִּית, and רַעֲשָׁנִים.

Notice how the melody shifts when the scene changes from the rowdy Purim to the peaceful Shabbat. (This melody is a variation of that used in the song "*Shabbat Shalom*" on this cassette tape.) Have the appropriate props here for the Rabbi — a kipah and tallit. The punch line "לֹא כָּל יוֹם פּוּרִים" is a common Israeli expression that means special events or circumstances do not occur every day.

5. "Four New Questions for the Seder"/ "מִי בְּסֵדֶר פֶּסַח?": *Kadimah!*, Unit 4; *Z'man Likro*, Lesson 16.

This song teaches the questions words: מַה and מִי as well as Pesach vocabulary. You might want to reinforce this song around Pesach time. Prepare two separate posters to illustrate *who* is at the Seder table and *what* is on it. Go over each of the vocabulary words. Act out the final question of *where* is the afikoman. The first time you sing the song, demonstrate searching for the afikoman in the places mentioned in the song. When students have mastered the vocabulary, ask for a volunteer to "conduct the search."

The song has a fairly quick tempo and *Kadimah!* students may have a hard time catching on to all of the words. Therefore, the posters that you made are particularly useful in teaching this song. You can give *Z'man Likro* students word sheets.

6. "Hello, Goodbye"/"שָׁלוֹם, שָׁלוֹם": *Z'man Likro*, Lesson 13.

This song introduces the three meanings of the word "Shalom," probably the most best known and most commonly used Hebrew word. Ask students if they know what the word means. Use picture illustrations and/or mime to demonstrate the multiple meanings of Shalom: hello, good-bye, and peace. Since the song lyrics are: "In every place we always say, 'Shalom,'" have students draw pictures of Jews from various countries saying "Shalom" to one another. Make a class bulletin board entitled "תָּמִיד אוֹמְרִים שָׁלוֹם."

7. "Time To Read Hebrew"/"זְמַן לִקְרֹא". Reprise.